RULERS,
SCHOLARS, AND
ARTISTS OF THE
RENAISSANCE™

GALILEO GALILEI | Father of
Modern Science

RULERS,
SCHOLARS, AND
ARTISTS OF THE
RENAISSANCE™

GALILEO GALILEI | Father of Modern Science

Rachel Hilliam

The Rosen Publishing Group, Inc., New York

In memory of Maurice Sewell

Published in 2005 by The Rosen Publishing Group, Inc.
29 East 21st Street, New York, NY 10010

First Edition

Library of Congress Cataloging-in-Publication Data

Hilliam, Rachel.
Galileo Galilei: father of modern science/Rachel Hilliam.—1st ed.
    p. cm.—(Rulers, scholars, and artists of the Renaissance)
Includes bibliographical references and index.
ISBN 1-4042-0314-1 (library binding)
1. Galilei, Galileo, 1564–1642—Juvenile literature.
2. Astronomers—Italy—Biography—Juvenile literature.
3. Physicists—Italy—Biography—Juvenile literature.
I. Title. II. Series.
QB36.G2H53 2005
520'.92—dc22

2004008748

Manufactured in the United States of America

On the cover: The Leaning Tower of Pisa. Inset: Galileo Galilei.

CONTENTS

ITALY AT THE TIME OF GALILEO GALILEI

Padua • • Venice

Pisa •   • Florence
         • Siena

         • Rome

INTRODUCTION: FATHER OF MODERN SCIENCE

In 1972, when the astronauts David Scott and Jim Irwin from *Apollo 15* landed on the Moon, they simultaneously dropped a feather and a hammer, then watched to see which would fall faster. Our instincts tell us that the hammer would fall faster, but about 370 years prior, Galileo Galilei had predicted they would fall to the ground at exactly the same time. Indeed, when Scott dropped the objects this is exactly what happened. Then, in 1989, NASA launched the *Galileo* probe to discover more about the planet Jupiter. The mission lasted six years and many new observations were made about Jupiter, again, based on those first described by Galileo. These two endeavors are a direct result of Galileo's work. His ideas of motion were far beyond his time, as

Galileo established mechanics as a science. He was the first to put forth the ideas of force as a mechanical agent and the invariability in the relation of cause and effect.

were his observations of the solar system. But perhaps most important, he changed the way scientists worked by conducting experiments to test ideas.

Still in existence are the five most important books Galileo wrote during his lifetime, two of his original hand-made telescopes, and more than 2,000 letters he wrote to various friends and correspondents. All these bits of evidence help us construct a picture of Galileo's life and works.

Galileo Galilei (1564–1642) lived at a time in history known as the Renaissance. This was a period in Europe of increased interest in learning and the arts. Paintings and sculptures were produced with a degree of skill that had not been seen since the time of ancient Greece and Rome. In fact, the word "renaissance" means "rebirth." Artists in Italy could see the remains of the past around them and were inspired to replicate them. Great artists such as Michelangelo (1475–1564) and in particular Leonardo da Vinci (1452–1519) were also interested in science. They represented an emerging group of intellectuals who were prepared to challenge the teachings of the past, along with the teachings of Italian universities and the Roman Catholic Church.

During the Renaissance, the universities in Italy based their teachings on the works of the ancient Greek philosopher Aristotle (384–322 BC). Although Aristotle lived before the founding of Christianity, the Catholic Church respected his views, which did not go against the biblical understanding of the universe. The Catholic Church was very powerful during the Renaissance, so criticizing Aristotle was almost the same as criticizing the church. Criticism of the church was considered a crime and could result in harsh punishment, such as being burned at the stake. Aristotle believed that the planets moved around Earth, which remained stationary. The Catholic Church adopted this belief.

The observations Galileo made of the solar system seemed to suggest that Earth was not stationary, but in fact revolved around the Sun, contrary to the teachings of the Catholic Church. Galileo could not have imagined the trouble these observations would

Galileo demonstrates his telescope to the Senate of Venice. Although they are clearly observing the stars here, in reality the senators were immediately impressed with the military potential of the invention for observance of ships approaching the Venetian ports.

cause him. Though he is often thought of as the scientist who challenged the established teachings of the church, he was in fact a devout Catholic who had once thought about becoming a monk.

However, the most important contribution Galileo made to science was the concept of performing accurate experiments that could be repeated. Today, scientists make an observation of the world around them, formulate a hypothesis, or question, about the observation, and then test the hypothesis using a repeatable experiment. Before Galileo's time, people tried to understand how the world worked by logic and reason. Aristotle's teachings were accepted as the truth, but no one actually bothered to test whether the hypotheses he made were correct. For example, people believed that if two stones of different weights were dropped, the heavier one would fall to the ground first. We shall see that this is not the case, but Galileo was the first person to actually perform an experiment to test the idea. This was the beginning of modern science as we know it. He paved the way for future great scientists such as Sir Isaac Newton (1643–1727) and Albert Einstein (1879–1955). For this, Galileo can truly be called the Father of Modern Science.

GALILEO'S EARLY LIFE

Galileo Galilei was born in Pisa, Italy, on February 15, 1564, the same year the English playwright William Shakespeare was born and the Italian artist Michelangelo died. Galileo's odd-sounding name was due to a fifteenth-century ancestor, Galileo Bonaiuti. He was Galileo's great-great-uncle and had been a well-respected physician and chief magistrate. The family changed its surname to Galilei in his honor and Galileo was also given his first name.

Galileo's father, Vincenzio Galilei, was born in Florence, Italy, in 1520, and had a significant influence on his son. He studied music in Venice and later made his living as a composer, singer, teacher, and lute player. Vincenzio published several books on music theory and musical scores for

A view of the River Arno, which runs through Pisa, the birthplace of Galileo. Pisa had been a major center of trade, prospering from its location on the sea until the fifteenth century. By that time, silt deposits from the Arno had cut if off from the shoreline, bringing about a decline in trade. Florence captured the city in 1509.

the lute. He also performed several experiments using mathematics to try to explain how musical instruments worked. For example, if a scale of eight notes is played, the top and bottom of the scale are one octave apart. If this scale was played on a string instrument, for example a lute, it was thought that the tension in the top string of the scale was twice as much as the bottom string. Vincenzio conducted experiments that involved hanging weights from these strings to show that, in fact, the top string had a tension four times greater than the bottom string.

These experiments probably had a strong influence on Galileo.

Vincenzio settled in Pisa around 1560 and married Giulia Ammannati in 1563. She gave birth to seven children, of which Galileo (1564) was the eldest. Three of these children appear to have died in infancy, leaving Galileo financially responsible for his siblings Virginia (1573), Michelangelo (1575), and Livia (1587) when his father died in 1591.

Vincenzio supplemented his income by dealing in textiles with a local businessman named Muzio Tedaldi. In 1572, when Galileo was eight years old, his father decided to return to Florence and left Galileo with Tedaldi. Vincenzio became a musician in the Florentine court, which meant that his family mingled with dukes and princes and often spent time at their residences. Tuscany, of which Florence was the capital, flourished in the Renaissance as a center of learning and the arts.

HISTORY OF ITALY AND TUSCANY

It wasn't until the 1860s that Italy would again be unified for the first time since the fall of the Roman Empire in the late fifth century. In those intervening years, including the Renaissance, the

Ignazio Danti (1536–1586) was a Dominican priest who was ordered by Cosimo I de' Medici, in power at the time of Galileo's birth, to prepare maps for his palazzo. Danti then became a famous cartographer and surveyor. He created this fresco of Italy, which can be found in the map room of the Palazzo Vecchio in Florence, with cartographer and Olivetan monk Stefano Buonsignori.

Cosimo I de' Medici, who was ruling Florence at the time of Galileo's birth, restored the power of the great ruling family during the waning years of the Renaissance.

country evolved as a group of independently ruled regions.

Galileo was born under the rule of Cosimo I de' Medici, a member of the powerful Medici family that held power in Florence almost continuously from 1434 until 1737. Cosimo had been given the title grand duke of Tuscany in 1570. Though he died when Galileo was ten years old, his descendants would remain in power until 1737.

With the Medicis' patronage, arts and literature flourished. It was important for the success of the Galilei family to have the patronage of the Medici family.

GALILEO'S SCHOOLING

Galileo joined the rest of his family in Florence when he was ten years old and was taught music and mathematics by his father with the help of a tutor named Jacopo Borghini. Although Galileo became an accomplished lute player, he had no wish to follow his father's musical career. He began school at the age of eleven in a monastery at Vallombrosa, southeast of Florence.

At the age of fifteen, Galileo joined the monastery as a novice. His father, although he was Catholic, was horrified, since he had already decided his eldest son should become a doctor. When Galileo developed an eye infection, Vincenzio was able to remove him from the monastery in order to see a doctor in Florence. Though Galileo's eye recovered, he never returned to the monastery. Instead, he continued his education at a school run by monks. Since this was located in Florence, he lived at home where Vincenzio could keep watch over him.

GALILEO'S STUDIES AT THE UNIVERSITY OF PISA

In 1581, Vincenzio sent his son back to Pisa, where he lived again with Muzio Tedaldi. This time he enrolled at the University of Pisa as a medical student. Galileo never took his medical studies seriously, and in 1583, he met Ostilio Ricci, the mathematician to the grand duke of Tuscany. One day he

A view of the Arno and Pisa as they are today. Much of the city still retains its medieval architecture. Also, due to the sandy soil upon which it was built, the city is known to have other leaning edifices besides the famous Leaning Tower.

went to visit his new friend and found him giving a mathematics lecture to some students. The subject interested him so much that he joined the students on an informal basis for the mathematics course. During the summer of 1583, Galileo invited Ricci to his home, where Ricci tried to persuade Vincenzio to allow Galileo to study mathematics. His father was strongly opposed to the idea, since jobs for doctors were far more plentiful than mathematics posts. This did not deter Galileo from attending mathematics lectures rather than his medical studies.

All university teaching at the time was based on books written by the ancient Greek philosopher Aristotle. This had been the case since the twelfth century, when Aristotle's works were translated from Greek and Arabic to Latin. Aristotle was considered to have the answers to all questions concerning the universe.

As a student, Galileo was unafraid to question the teachings of Aristotle. For example, Galileo argued against Aristotle's theory on motion. Aristotle believed there was no cause without an effect, in other words, everything that happens is the result of some action. When this theory is applied to moving bodies, it means that there is no motion without a force. If this is true, the speed of a moving body is proportional to the force moving it, and inversely proportional to resistance against it. For example, when you push a buggy, the buggy moves so long as you are pushing it, but as soon as you stop pushing, the buggy will stop. If this principle is applied to falling

19

Most of Aristotle's surviving work is in the form of lecture notes that were not intended for publication. Even so, this work made an enormous impact on Western intellectual and scientific traditions.

bodies, the force is the weight pulling the body down and the resistance is the substance it falls through, such as air or water. So if Aristotle was right and weight determines speed, when two bodies of different weights are dropped at the same time, the heavier of the two must fall faster. Galileo argued this could not be the case, since he had observed hailstones of different sizes reach the ground at the same time. According to Aristotle, this must mean the lighter hailstones came from a lower cloud than the heavier hailstones. Wouldn't a simpler explanation be that all the hailstones came from the same place and therefore fall at the same speed regardless of their weight? It would be later in Galileo's life that he showed this to be the case.

Though Galileo spent so much time on his mathematical studies rather than his medical studies, his father refused to let him change course. Since he was still officially enrolled as a medical student, he left the University of Pisa in 1585 without a degree in any subject!

THE PENDULUM

One popular story about Galileo's student days at the University of Pisa took place in the Cathedral of Pisa. During what was a particularly boring sermon, Galileo became interested in the cathedral's chandelier. As it swung in the breeze, the chandelier traced part of the circumference of a circle, or an arc. Galileo noticed that the time taken for a complete swing appeared to stay the same whether the arc was small or large. Accurate clocks were not available in Galileo's day, so he needed some other method of measurement in order to test his observation. To do this, it is said that he used his pulse and counted how many beats each swing took. Whether this story is true is open to question, as with many stories about Galileo, but what is true is that his interest in the swing of the pendulum started about this time.

About twenty years later, Galileo began serious investigations into pendulums. He went on to show that not only does the time taken for a complete swing remain the same for different arc lengths, but it also remains constant for pendulums of different weights. In fact, the only factor that affects the pendulum's swing time is the length of the pendulum. It is amusing to think that if Galileo really did use his pulse to time the swings, it was this discovery that led to the development of the first accurate clocks!

WORKS ON MOTION

After leaving the University of Pisa, Galileo returned to his father's house in Florence. For the next four years, he tried to make a living as a private tutor in mathematics and philosophy in both Florence and Siena.

In 1586, Galileo wrote his first scientific book, *La Bilancetta* (The Little Balance). The book began by describing the "Eureka" story, which was well-known in Galileo's day. It revolves around the problem given to Archimedes (287–212 BC), an ancient Greek mathematician and physicist, by Hieron, the king of Syracuse. The story is about a goldsmith who had been given a certain amount of gold to make a crown for the king. When it was finished, the king thought that the goldsmith had mixed the gold with a less precious metal and cheated him out of

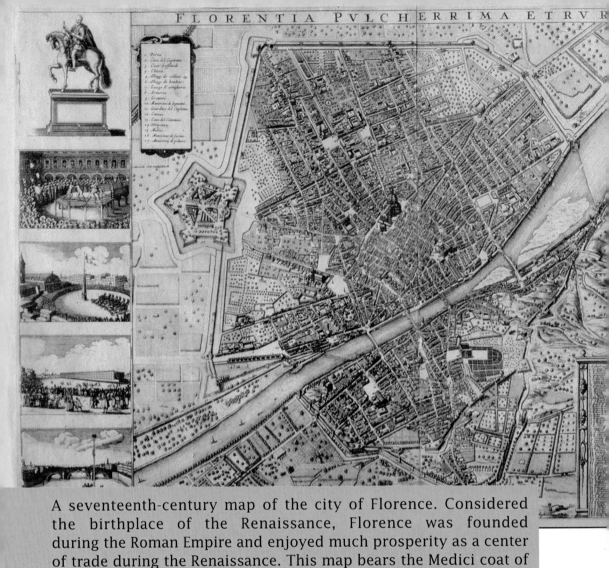

A seventeenth-century map of the city of Florence. Considered the birthplace of the Renaissance, Florence was founded during the Roman Empire and enjoyed much prosperity as a center of trade during the Renaissance. This map bears the Medici coat of arms in the upper right-hand corner.

his gold. If a metal such as silver had been added, the crown would weigh the same amount but would be bulkier since silver is less dense than gold. Archimedes is said to have been in the public baths when he realized that for his body to be immersed in the pool, a quantity of water equal to the bulk of his body must overflow from the baths. Upon this discovery, he supposedly rushed naked from the baths

shouting, "Eureka, Eureka," meaning, "I've found it, I've found it!" By applying this reasoning to the crown problem, Archimedes was able to measure how much water overflowed when a mass of silver equal to the weight of the crown was placed in a vessel and how much overflowed when a mass of gold equal to that of the crown was placed in a vessel. When he put the crown in, he found that it displaced more water than the gold, but less than the silver, so he was able to conclude that the crown was a mixture of both metals.

Galileo extended this idea to produce an accurate balance for weighing material in air and water. His balance consisted of an arm wrapped with metal wire on which a counterweight was hung from one end. To measure the weight of a piece of metal, the wire could be turned to move the counterweight until the balance was level. The number of turns required to do this in water could then be counted, and the weight of one metal in relation to the counterweight could be accurately measured.

The following year, Galileo traveled to Rome to discuss geometry with Christoph Clavius, a professor

Christoph Clavius was the chief mathematician who engineered the reformation of the Gregorian calendar in 1582. The esteemed astronomer and mathematician was revered by Galileo, as well as Johannes Kepler and Tycho Brahe.

of mathematics at the Jesuit Collegio Romano. Jesuits were considered the most learned group in the Catholic Church, and it was important for Galileo's future career not only to have the support of noble men, but also the support of the church. Galileo impressed Clavius so much that Clavius encouraged him to apply for the chair of mathematics at the University of Bologna in 1588. He was unfortunately turned down for the position, but his work interested Marquis Guidobaldo del Monte, the author of an important book on mechanics, *Liber mechanicorum* (1577). Galileo kept in regular correspondence with both Clavius and del Monte for many years.

As Galileo's name became known, he was invited to give two lectures at the Florentine Academy on the arrangement, dimension, and location of hell in

Dante's *Inferno*. The Italian poet Dante Alighieri (1265–1321) had included the science of the time into his famous poem *The Divine Comedy*. His description of hell, or "the inferno," was so detailed that it seemed scientifically correct. During the sixteenth century, it was a popular subject for debate.

These lectures, together with Clavius and del Monte's support, secured Galileo the position of chair in mathematics at the University of Pisa when it became vacant in 1589. The official syllabus at the university, which Galileo faithfully followed, was based on Aristotle. In private, however, Galileo's discussions took new turns. Although his position as chair was a highly regarded one, the pay was still low, so Galileo had to supplement his income by privately tutoring pupils. These students, sons of the rich and powerful, lived with him full time, which meant that Galileo's fame spread when these students returned home and spoke of their tutor.

EXPERIMENTS WITH FALLING BODIES

Another story, which has probably been embellished over time, involves Galileo's climb up the Leaning Tower of Pisa to throw cannonballs from the top. According to Aristotelian physics, objects of different weights fall at different speeds. This means that

Audiences were impressed with Galileo's assessment that Lucifer was 2,000 arm-lengths long. This was his interpretation of Dante's description of the beast Nimrod in Canto 31 of *The Inferno*. Ironically, his analysis of this literary work helped him obtain his first teaching post. Above is a depiction by Gustave Doré of the giant Antaeus from Canto 31.

according to Aristotle, a 100-pound (45-kilogram) ball falling from a height of 328 feet (100 meters) would hit the ground before a 1-pound (0.45-kg) ball has fallen 3.28 feet (1 m). When the balls were supposedly thrown from the tower, the larger one did hit the ground first, but only by a fraction of a second, due to what we now know to be air resistance. This did not deter Galileo's opponents from pointing out that his prediction had been wrong.

DISCOVERIES ABOUT MOTION

Late in 1586, Galileo started to write about problems of motion. During the three years Galileo was at Pisa (1589–1592), he revised this work into a formal series of essays called *De Motu* (On Motion), which included several attacks on Aristotle's physics. These were never published, as he was probably not satis-fied with them since they contain some errors. However, one of the most important new

Here, two stone balls approximately the same size as those allegedly used by Galileo in his experiment on falling bodies are placed at a plat-form's edge on the Leaning Tower of Pisa. According to legend, students and scholars gathered below the tower to observe the experiment that would disprove Aristotle.

ideas in the essay was the concept that it is possible to test theories by taking measurements. Galileo built a sloping surface down which he could roll balls. He placed threads across the slope with bells attached to them, which would sound whenever a ball hit them. By listening to the intervals between the chimes of the

The acceleration stage of motion had largely been ignored by Aristotle and his followers. When Galileo rolled a metal ball down the groove of a wooden, sloped surface, he showed the rate of acceleration.

bells, he was able to determine how the speed of the balls changed.

In 1604, he returned to this work and formulated the correct law of falling bodies, which states that in a vacuum, all bodies, regardless of their weight, shape, or specific gravity, are uniformly accelerated in exactly the same way. He also showed that the distance fallen is proportional to the square of the elapsed time, so that if a ball falls one unit of distance in one unit of time, it will then fall four units of distance in two units of time and then nine units of distance in three units of time, and so on. By adjusting the sloping surface from shallow inclines to steep ones, he was able to show that the relationship was always true.

He would return to this work throughout his life. In 1608, he proved that a projectile follows a parabolic path. This means that when a cannon is fired or an object is thrown in the air, the path of the object is a bell-shaped curve. People at that time believed that a cannonball would fly in a straight line and then suddenly fall vertically to the ground. Galileo not only observed this was not the case, but mathematically proved what the curve was and showed that it was the same regardless of the weight of the object in question. He also showed that if the cannonball hit its target at the same height as it was fired, the speed at which it hit the target must be the same as the speed it left the cannon.

These results, together with many others, formed part of Galileo's final book, *Discourses and Mathematical Demonstrations Concerning Two New Sciences*. When the English scientist Isaac Newton read the English translation of this book, published in 1661, he made various notes that would later help him establish his own laws of universal gravitation in 1666.

When Vincenzio Galilei died in 1591, Galileo, as the eldest son, was left to provide financial support for the rest of his family. Together with his younger brother, Michelangelo Galilei, he was now responsible for paying the dowry promised to his newly married sister, Virginia. With this additional financial demand, Galileo set out to secure the better-paying position of chair of mathematics at the University of Padua in the Venetian Republic. To help his application, he visited the court at Venice and made a good impression on a wealthy intellectual named Gianvincenzio Pinelli as well as General Francesco del Monte, the younger brother of Guidobaldo who had encouraged him to apply for the position at Bologna. These people helped him secure the job initially for four years. However Galileo, then twenty-eight, was to remain in this post for the next eighteen years.

MECHANICAL INVENTIONS

CHAPTER 3

Galileo was appointed to the chair of mathematics at the University of Padua in 1592, at a time when the city came under Venetian rule. Galileo's early work at the university was of a practical nature. He offered private courses in military architecture, fortification, surveying, and mechanics to young foreign noblemen who were enrolled at the university with the intention of following a military career. With these students in mind, he wrote an essay on military fortifications that included sighting and triangulation that would also be of importance to the Venetian Republic.

Galileo was constantly trying to find ways to enhance his income by inventing something. An early idea was a thermometer, consisting of a glass tube that was open at one end

A view of the Ducal Palace—the seat of Venetian government—and the pier in Venice. Venice's population during Galileo's time was around 150,000. The hub between Europe and the East, Venice's powerful navy gained control of trade routes of the Mediterranean Sea.

and was sealed at the other. The idea was to heat the tube and then place the open end in a bowl of water to cool. As the air in the bulb cooled, it contracted, taking up less space so that the water was sucked partly up the tube. Changes in temperature could then be measured using the height of the liquid. When the sealed end was cooler, the water went higher up the tube. Since the height of the liquid also depended on the changing pressure of the air outside, the invention was not a great success.

THE GEOMETRIC AND MILITARY COMPASS

Galileo did hit on one moneymaking idea in 1597. Following his tutelage of military students, he invented a device he called the geometric and military compass. As the cannon became more movable, instruments were developed by other scientists to measure the elevation of the barrel. A gunner's compass was also developed in the sixteenth century, consisting of two arms at right angles with a circular scale between them holding a plumb line to indicate the elevations. Galileo combined all these instruments into one proportional compass, and by 1599 had refined the instrument, which had many useful scales engraved on its legs for a variety of purposes. It became the equivalent of a pocket calculator and could give the approximate solution to any mathematical problem likely to arise in those days, including determining the proper charge for any size of cannon and calculating square roots and exchange rates for money.

Galileo initially made these instruments himself, but demand became so great that by July 1599, he employed an instrument maker by the name of Marcantonio Mazzoleni, who came to live with him.

This meant that Galileo was unable to keep all the profits for himself. However, he charged every military student for instruction in using the compass. Having initially written the instruction manual as a learning aid, a few years later he published the booklet for sale with the instrument, thus generating yet more income. However there was no way of preventing other people from making the instrument or passing on their knowledge of how to use it, so this successful venture certainly did not secure his fortune.

THE TELESCOPE

Galileo first heard about the telescope in the summer of 1609. It had been possible since the thirteenth century to use lenses to magnify objects, and spectacles to correct both long- and shortsighted vision were readily available. In October 1608, a Dutch spectacle-maker by the name of Hans Lippershey realized it was possible to put a convex and concave lens in a tube

Here, Galileo's compass *(top)* and several depictions of its uses show how handy the instrument was for gunners. Not only could they elevate the cannon more accurately, they could quickly calculate how much gunpowder was needed for cannonballs of different sizes and materials.

and produce a magnification of four times greater than the human eye alone. News of this invention spread around Europe, and by April 1609, the spy-glasses were sold as toys in several spectacle-makers' shops in Paris. However, it was Galileo who would make the telescope famous. Hearing about these toys, he realized they could be put to use for both military and trade purposes, particularly in Venice, where it was necessary to identify ships approaching the port.

Galileo at last thought he had an idea that would solve his money problems. However, in August 1609, while he was still in Venice, news reached Galileo that a Dutchman had taken one of these instruments to Padua. He rushed back only to discover that the stranger was now in Venice and was trying to sell the instrument to the doge, or magistrate. Knowing this object could solve his financial problems, he set about trying to re-create the invention with only the knowledge that the telescope consisted of two lenses. Within twenty-four hours, he had produced the best telescope of the day. While the Dutch version consisted of two concave lenses, which produced an upside-down image, Galileo's version had one convex and one concave lens and therefore gave an upright image.

On August 4, Friar Paolo Sarpi, the adviser to the Senate in Venice (and a close friend of Galileo's), received a coded message explaining Galileo's success.

The decision of what to do with the Dutch instrument was therefore delayed, giving Galileo time to build a telescope with ten times the magnification power! He traveled to Venice with this instrument at the end of August and demonstrated its powers to the doge and Senate. With Galileo's telescope, they were able to see boats coming into port two hours before they could be seen by the naked eye. Galileo

Galileo recounted the events of his race to invent the telescope with the arrival of the foreign salesman to the Venetian Republic in *Sidereus Nuncius* (The Starry Messenger). It was through these telescopes in 1610 that Galileo would discover Jupiter's moons.

offered the telescope as a gift to the doge, who, in return, renewed Galileo's post at the University of Padua for life and doubled his salary. Galileo accepted the offer, even though it meant he would be burdened with considerable teaching duties.

He continued to refine his instrument and by December 1609, had produced an instrument that could magnify objects by a factor of twenty. In later

life, Galileo used his knowledge of lenses to produce an effective compound microscope. This consisted of two lenses with a doubly convex shape (curved on both sides). This special shape was difficult to produce, but Galileo managed to ground the lens for this instrument. His microscope, along with his telescopes, considered the best in the world at the time, show Galileo's skill not only as a scientist, but also as a craftsman. Using the microscope, he drew detailed illustrations of insects, which were published in Rome in 1625. The part Galileo played in the microscope's invention is often overlooked due to his other achievements and the fact that the full use of the instrument was not recognized until much later.

Galileo did not invent the microscope. However, after becoming acquainted with the compound microscope, he introduced some improvements to its construction.

FAMILY LIFE

CHAPTER 4

In his later years, Galileo would look back on his time at Padua (1592–1610) as one of the happiest of his life. This was due partly to the circle of friends he acquired. Pinelli, who had helped Galileo secure the job, often invited the Paduan lecturers to meet dignitaries and other scholars who were visiting his house. Galileo lodged with him for a brief time and remained a close friend. Galileo probably met Friar Paolo Sarpi and Cardinal Roberto Bellarmine through Pinelli.

Sarpi became a close personal friend of Galileo's. Though he was appointed the official theologian to the Republic of Venice, he held unconventional views on religion and was an enthusiastic student of philosophy and science. It was Sarpi to whom Galileo had first written in 1604 about

In Renaissance Italy, people met in town squares and other public areas to discuss the latest scientific discoveries and exciting works of art. This is a view of such a scene on the Palazzo Vecchio in Florence.

his work on falling objects and to whom he sent the coded message concerning his telescope in 1609. Bellarmine was a theologian and intellectual who was a leading figure in the Catholic Church.

It is interesting that these two men were such close friends of Galileo's as they held widely differing views. Sarpi was a constant problem for Pope Paul V, who had been elected in 1605. Sarpi argued that the way to heaven was through spiritual works and did not believe that popes and kings had the right to exercise political power in the name of God. On the opposite side of the argument, Bellarmine was the main advocate of this right. Because of the increased tension between Venice and the pope, the doge and all his officials, including Sarpi, were excommunicated in 1606. Sarpi was invited to Rome to argue his political views with

S.ROBERTVS CARD. BELLARMINVS.
E SOC. IESV.
MARCELLI. II. P. M. NEPOS.

Cardinal Roberto Bellarmine was a strong defender of papal power, often finding himself in the center of controversies, defending this divine right of the pope. Scholarly works by him influenced many people away from Protestantism and back to the Catholic Church.

Bellarmine but refused the invitation with the backing of the Venetian Senate. In response, the Vatican burned all Sarpi's books, which only served to make Sarpi's influence in the republic stronger.

Though Galileo enjoyed an active social life, the consequences of one event would affect him for the rest of his life. During the summer of 1603, he visited a nearby villa with a group of friends. Having had a walk and a large meal, the friends went for their afternoon siesta in an underground room. The natural air-conditioning cooled the room using a pipe that delivered wind from a waterfall inside a nearby mountain cave. The pipe was closed when the three friends went to sleep but opened later by a servant. It seems that poisonous gases from the caves may have entered the room, leaving all three men very ill, to the extent that one later died. Though Galileo survived, he was often confined to bed for long periods of time throughout the rest of his life.

MARINA GAMBA

Another reason for Galileo's fond memories of his time in Padua was his relationship with Marina Gamba. No one is sure exactly how the two met. Although they never married, they had a stable and widely acknowledged relationship for twelve years. Gamba lived in Venice where Galileo made frequent visits. At the age of twenty-two, she gave birth to their first child, Virginia, in 1600. Gamba went on to have two more children, Livia Antonia in 1601, and Vincenzio Andrea in 1606. It was traditional in those days for scholars to remain single since this meant they could work as they wanted with no ties. Gamba was also from a lower class than Galileo, making it difficult for Galileo to marry her. However, even after Marina Gamba married Giovanni Bartoluzzi in 1613, Galileo still remained friends with both of them and even helped Bartoluzzi find employment.

GALILEO'S CHILDREN

In the same year that his daughter Virginia was born, Galileo's youngest sister, Livia, married, leaving Galileo with a second large dowry to pay. In 1608, his brother married, moved to Germany, and refused to pay his share of the two dowries. This led to legal action from his first brother-in-law, Benedetto Landucci. Luckily Giovanfrancesco Sagredo, a Venetian nobleman and friend of Galileo's, paid the court fees and delayed the legal process, giving Galileo time to argue his case.

Since Galileo's two daughters were illegitimate, finding suitable husbands for them would have been problematic even if he had been able to meet the large dowries required for his daughters to marry suitors appropriate to his social standing. He therefore took steps to secure their admission to a nearby convent, although at ages eleven and ten they were far too young to take religious vows. Galileo wrote to Francesco Maria Cardinal del Monte, who had helped with his first teaching appointment in Pisa, asking if it was possible to have the girls admitted. He was informed that he must wait until at least one of them reached the required age of sixteen. However, Galileo kept trying, and in 1613, he received permission through the office of Cardinal Maffeo Barberini for Virginia, now thirteen, and Livia, age twelve, to be admitted to the Convent of San Matteo in Arcetri.

SISTER MARIA CELESTE

On October 4, 1616, Galileo's first daughter, Virginia, became a nun and was given the name Sister Maria Celeste, three years after she had entered the convent. Her younger sister followed her actions the next year and became Sister Arcangela. There are about 120 surviving letters from Maria Celeste to Galileo written between 1623 and 1633, giving a good picture of her personality and her life at San Matteo. This is an excerpt from a letter dated October 20, 1623:

> I enclose herewith a little composition, which, aside from expressing to you the

Galileo's oldest daughter, Sister Maria Celeste, was devoted to her father, even performing the salutary penance for him—reciting of seven psalms once a week—that was his punishment after his trial. She suffered from chronic illness and died on April 2, 1634.

extent of our need, will also give you the excuse to have a hearty laugh at the expense of my foolish writing; but because I have seen how good-naturedly you always encourage my meager intelligence, Sire, you have lent me the courage to attempt this essay. Indulge me then, Lord Father, and with your usual loving tenderness please help us.

Maria's letters to Galileo often asked her father for financial aid for the convent, and he always seemed happy to help. He supplied the convent with many items, including thread for sewing. He also chose organ music for them and gave gifts of food, including his homegrown citrus fruits, wine, and rosemary leaves. In addition, he mended their clocks and seems to have been highly regarded in the convent.

Throughout her life, Maria Celeste was quick to help Galileo in any way possible and would often copy letters for him; undertake sewing, washing, and bleaching collars; and concoct potions for his ailments. This was alongside her convent duties, of which prayer occupied a large part. The nuns at San Matteo grew fruits and vegetables, did their own cooking and cleaning, and made articles for sale, including herbal medicine, embroidered handkerchiefs, lace, and bread. Maria Celeste was the apothecary for the convent and because she had inherited the family's musical talents, she also directed the convent choir.

THE MEDICI FAMILY

Galileo's fortunes were linked to the Medici family throughout his life. Since his father had been a court musician, he had come into contact with the family from an early age. Cosimo I, who had employed Galileo's father, died when Galileo was ten years old. Cosimo's son, Francesco I, was not an effective ruler and met a sudden death at the age of forty-two. Power was handed to his brother Ferdinand I, age thirty-eight, in 1587. It was Ferdinand who had appointed Galileo to the University of Pisa in 1589, the same year Ferdinand had married the deeply religious Christina of Lorraine. Ferdinand and Christina had four sons and four daughters; the eldest son was Cosimo II.

In 1605, Chistina invited Galileo to instruct her son Cosimo in the use of his military compass and mathematics. This coincided with a trip to Florence when Galileo was trying to sort out legal affairs with his sisters' dowries. Though no formal contract

Here, Galileo is depicted showing Cosimo II his discovery of the satellites of Jupiter. Galileo dedicated the discovery to Cosimo, and although he wanted to name them the Cosmian Stars, his patron preferred him to call the satellites the Medicean Stars, which is how they became known.

existed between Galileo and the Medici household, it was assumed that Galileo would give instruction to Cosimo as and when required. It was to Cosimo at the age of sixteen that Galileo dedicated his essay on the military compass. When Cosimo married Maria Maddalena in 1608, Galileo was again summoned by

Christina to oversee work on a large wooden stage in the middle of the River Arno that would be the focus of the wedding celebrations.

In 1609, Christina consulted Galileo again. This time, her husband was very ill, and she asked Galileo to cast his horoscope. She did not seem to realize that Galileo was an astronomer and not an astrologer! Galileo predicted that Ferdinand would soon recover and live for many years. Unfortunately, Ferdinand died a few weeks later, and with this blunder it looked as though this was the end of any help the Medici family would give Galileo. Cosimo became His Serene Highness Grand Duke Cosimo II, sovereign of all Tuscany, at the age of nearly nineteen.

ASTRONOMICAL OBSERVATIONS

CHAPTER 5

In October 1604, Galileo observed a supernova, believing it to be a new star, using the surveying techniques he had used in his military work. Today we know that this observation was of a star dying and not a new star. An explosion takes place when the material from one star falls onto another nearby star. The mass of the second star increases so much that the matter inside the star is crushed and becomes hot enough to cause a huge explosion. When this happens, the star is about 100 million times brighter than the Sun. Galileo noticed that the star was always seen in the same place with respect to nearby fixed stars. The ancient Babylonians gave the term "constellations" to groups of fixed stars, which have no motion in relation to each other. According to

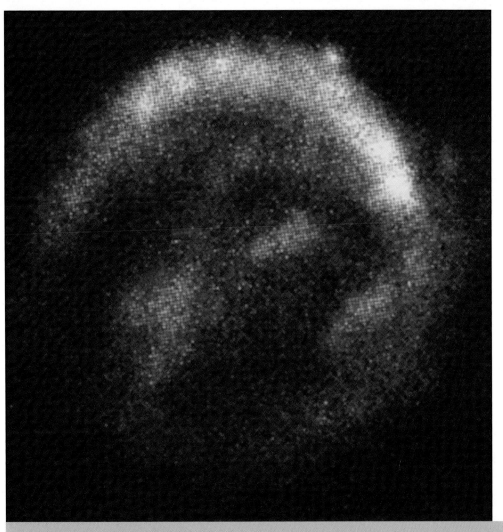

Now known as Kepler's supernova, after the esteemed German astronomer who studied the phenomenon starting October 17, 1604, this is the last supernova to be observed in our galaxy, the Milky Way. Galileo's first documented astronomical observation was of this supernova.

Aristotle, no change could take place in the heavens as everything in heaven was perfect, so no new star could appear. In the past, new stars had been explained as tails of motionless comets, which were closer to Earth than the fixed stars. Galileo gave a series of public lectures explaining how his

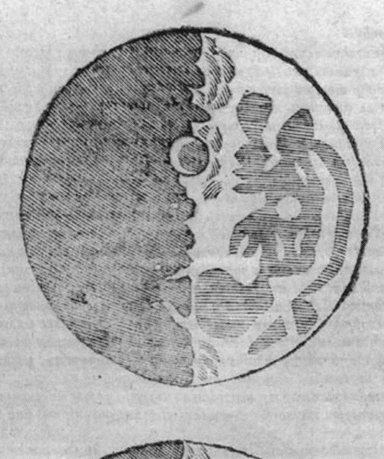

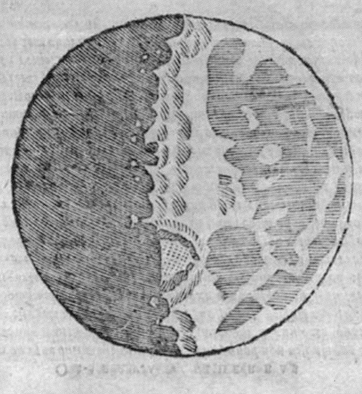

observations and careful measurements of angles placed this star as far away from Earth as other stars, disproving this Aristotelian notion.

In November 1609, he decided to use his newly made telescope to look at the heavens. With the increased magnification, he was able to make careful drawings of the Moon on each clear night for several months. He noticed that the dark lines defining the spots on the Moon changed in width, and he came to the conclusion that these lines must be the shadows of mountains and valleys on the surface. Aristotle had suggested that the Moon was a perfect sphere, but Galileo's discovery contradicted this.

SATELLITES OF JUPITER

As Galileo was finishing his observations of the Moon toward the end of 1609, Jupiter was the next brightest object in the sky. On January 7, 1610, Galileo noticed what he initially thought were three fixed stars near Jupiter. When he returned the following evening, he

At left are Galileo's drawings of his observations of the Moon. By demonstrating the irregularity of the Moon's surface, he concluded that indeed Earth was not unique in its terrain. This went against the teaching of the church that all heavenly bodies were smooth and perfect. Galileo also correctly calculated the height of the lunar mountains by the shadows they cast.

One of Jupiter's four Galilean satellites (named after their first observer) is Io, pictured here with its parent in the background. Io is approximately the same size as the Moon.

was expecting the stars to have been left behind since Jupiter was moving from east to west at this time. What he saw instead was that the stars were to the west of Jupiter. He continued observing the planet over the following weeks and by January 15, he had discovered there were four of these stars. Because of the movement, he realized that they must be planetary bodies revolving around Jupiter. The accepted view at the time was that everything revolved around Earth, but here were four bodies revolving around another planet.

Galileo quickly wrote down his discoveries in a new book, only fifty-six pages long, called *Sidereus*

This is a page from Galileo's manuscript, where he describes his observations of Jupiter's moons. After several days of observing, he concluded that these bodies revolved around Jupiter. His observations became one of the many attacks on Aristotelian cosmology, which stated that only Earth could be the center of motion.

Nuncius (The Starry Messenger), which was printed on March 13, 1610. Hoping to regain the favor of the Medici family, he dedicated this work again to Cosimo II, but this time went further and named the four new planets the Cosmian Stars. Cosimo preferred the name Medicean Stars and assigned one to himself and each of his three brothers.

Galileo had for some time wanted to return to his hometown of Pisa. By presenting the book along with his best telescope to Cosimo, he was appointed to the post of chief mathematician at the University of Pisa and philosopher and mathematician to the grand duke in 1610. The post was for life and the salary matched the increase he had been promised but not yet received from Venice. However, since he was also released from any further payments on Michelangelo's part of his two sisters' dowries, he really had a pay increase. Even better was the fact that he would no longer have any tiresome teaching duties.

PHASES OF VENUS

Just before Galileo left for Florence, he turned his telescope toward Saturn and noticed what he thought were two immobile moons. As he continued to observe Saturn, he noticed that sometimes the two "moons" seemed to disappear. What he was in fact seeing was

Saturn's ring system, which was not explained until 1657, by Dutchman Christian Huygens. When the rings are on edge, they are not visible, and though Galileo did not know this was what he was seeing, it was clear that Saturn was not a perfect sphere.

After Galileo moved to Florence, he began to study Venus and noticed that it seemed to show phases. Like the Moon, its appearance changed throughout the month. When Venus is at its furthest point from Earth, it looks like a perfectly round disk, but as it moves toward Earth, it appears to grow in size and is half illuminated, just like the Moon in the first and third quarters. When Venus is closest to Earth, it becomes invisible, just as the new Moon. These observations suggested that Venus must orbit the Sun. The more heavenly bodies Galileo observed, the more evidence he collected contradicting the perfect universe once described by Aristotle.

SUNSPOTS

Around this time, Galileo also observed dark spots on the face of the Sun, later called sunspots. A student of Galileo's named Benedetto Castelli had produced a safe method of viewing the Sun, by letting the reflection of the Sun fall on a screen placed behind the telescope. It was then possible to see

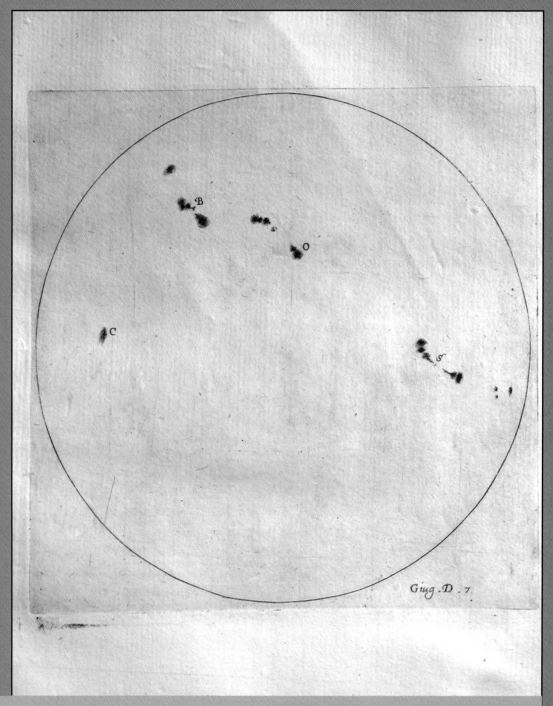

This is a drawing of sunspots made by Galileo on June 23, 1612. By observing the sunspots for a duration of several days, Galileo was able to conclude these were markings on the Sun's surface (and not planets) as well as estimate the Sun's rotation period.

the surface of the Sun clearly. As Galileo observed these dark spots, he noticed that they seemed to change. He noted the speed of the changes and realized that the Sun must rotate on its axis about once a month. These blemishes suggested that the Sun was also not a perfect sphere. Galileo was not aware that other astronomers had previously seen these spots. In particular, Christopher Scheiner, a German Jesuit professor, had argued that they were small satellites and that the Sun was therefore perfect. When Galileo found out about this, he strongly rejected Scheiner's suggestion and created a potential enemy as a result.

EVIDENCE FOR THE COPERNICAN SYSTEM

Aristotle had not only believed the Sun, stars, and other heavenly bodies were perfect spheres, but that each planet or star was attached to an invisible sphere that was centered on Earth. This meant that all the planets and stars would revolve in perfect circles around Earth. By using this method, a rough approximation to the position of each of the planets could be found. However, sometimes planets appear brighter and larger than at other times. This is because sometimes the planets are closer to Earth than at other times. For example, if the motion of Mars is studied, it appears to approach Earth from the west in April. This approach slows down in June when the planet then appears to move backward until mid-August when it starts moving east again. If all planets moved in perfect circles around Earth, this movement toward and away from Earth could not occur.

To account for this variation, Greek astronomer Claudius Ptolemy (AD 87–150) modified Aristotle's idea in his work *Almagest*. In his system, Earth remained fixed. Each planet was now attached to a small circle whose center was in turn placed on a larger carrying circle centered on Earth. This meant that the planets could move in loops and sometimes be closer to Earth than at other times. When these texts were translated into Latin, the Catholic Church accepted them, as they supported the church's belief that the perfect heaven Ptolemy described linked ideally with a perfect God.

Nicolaus Copernicus (1473–1543) was a Polish physician, lawyer, and church administrator who studied astronomy in his spare time. He published his life's work in *De Revolutionibus Orbium Coelestium* in 1543, the year of his death. In this book, he states that the Sun is the center of the universe, a system known as heliocentrism. This

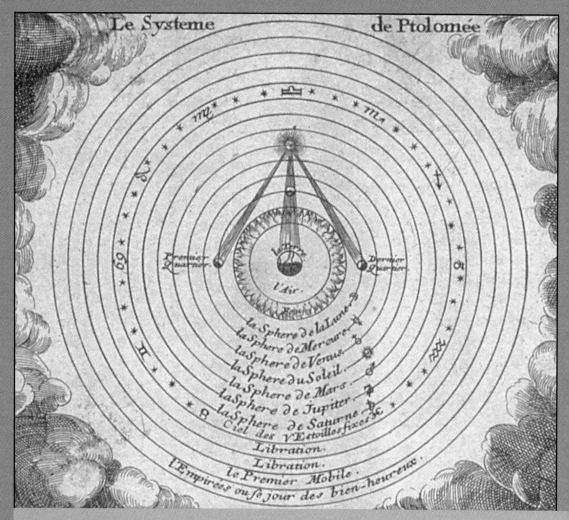

The universe, according to Ptolemy, was centered around a fixed Earth. The planets' motions were perfectly circular at a fixed speed. Also, according to Ptolemy, this cosmos was finite, meaning nothing existed outside of it.

system simplified the calculations needed to predict the motion of the planets. For example, Earth is the third planet from the Sun and Mars the fourth, so Earth will overtake the slower and more distant planet of Mars and naturally be sometimes closer to the planet and sometimes farther away. Copernicus did state, however, that the system was only a mathematical hypothesis and he had no proof that this was how the universe worked. A further system, introduced by the late sixteenth-century Danish astronomer Tycho Brahe (1546– 1601), was a mixture of heliocentrism and the Ptolemaic systems. This was called the Tychonic system and allowed the Moon and Sun to orbit Earth while the remaining planets orbited the Sun.

The motion of the universe may now seem obvious to us, but in those days, people could not accept the idea that Earth could revolve. After all, people asked, how would birds find their nests after they had left them if Earth did revolve? There was also a religious problem since a stationary Sun appeared to clash with several biblical passages. The church had no problem with using the Copernican system as a mathematical calculating tool, providing it was clear this was not what really happened in nature.

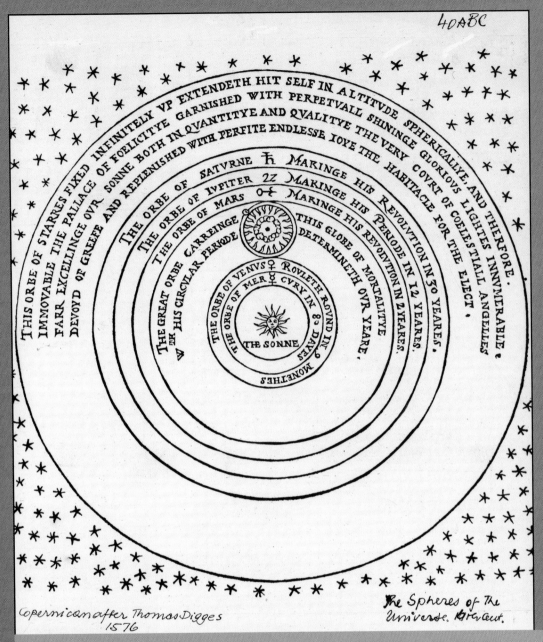

Copernican after Thomas Digges
1576

The Spheres of The
Universe. Bravant.

This depiction of the Copernican system was created by English astronomer Thomas Digges. Digges added an important feature in his illustration that was not realized at the time: the stars on the outside of the fixed sphere, representing heavenly bodies that extend to infinity.

It was against this background that Galileo began his astronomical observations. Each of his observations led him to believe that he really did live in a Copernican universe. For example, it had been argued if Earth really moved around the Sun, it would somehow lose the Moon, but Galileo's observation of the satellites of Jupiter showed that it was possible for Jupiter to move around another body (be it Earth or the Sun) without losing its satellites. In theory, it should also be possible for Earth to move. However, none of Galileo's observations provided concrete proof, since the Tychonic system could explain them all.

GALILEO IS HONORED IN ROME

There was growing disbelief in the observations Galileo claimed

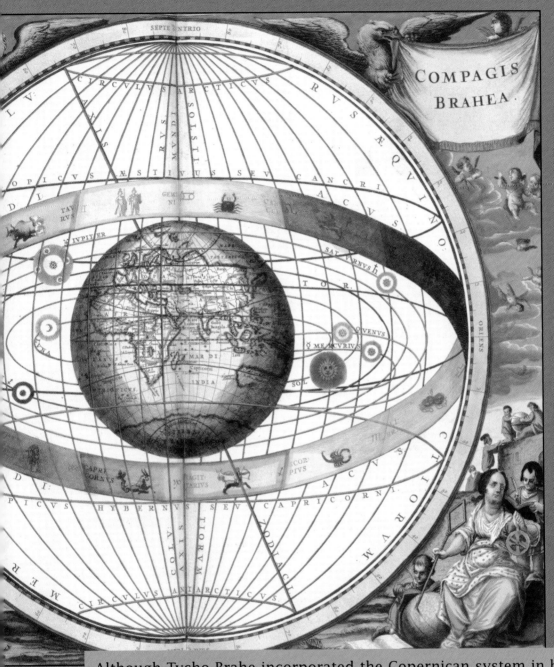

Although Tycho Brahe incorporated the Copernican system in his arrangement of the universe, he could not wholly embrace it because of his adherence to Aristotelian physics, with its fixed idea of place. Heavy bodies fall to their natural place—Earth. If Earth was not the center of the universe, than how else to explain this observed occurrence?

to have made. Some people even thought that his telescope lens must be defective, and therefore responsible for the images. In the hope of convincing more people he was right, Galileo set off for Rome in March 1611, as the scientific ambassador of the Tuscan state. The visit was a huge success and Galileo was granted a meeting with Pope Paul V. Galileo also met again both Cardinal Bellarmine and Father Clavius (the mathematician at the Jesuit Collegio Romano) who was now in his seventies. The Jesuits at the college honored him with a special conference and confirmed that all his observations were true. Attending this conference was the Marquis of Monticelli, Federico Cesi. Federico had established the world's first scientific society in 1603, the Lyncean Academy, to which he duly elected Galileo. This honor meant that Galileo could now add the title Lyncean after his signature. In addition, the academy also promised to become Galileo's publisher.

During this visit to Rome, Galileo also met Cardinal Maffeo Barberini, who would feature largely in his later life. When Galileo returned to Florence the following autumn, he met the cardinal again at a dinner party held by Grand Duke Cosimo II, on October 2, 1611. Galileo was the after-dinner entertainment and was to stage a debate about floating bodies with Vincenzio di Grazia, a philosophy professor from Pisa. At the time, people thought ice was denser than water and floated because it had a flat bottom. Galileo knew that ice was less dense than water and therefore always floated regardless of the shape. By placing the ice underwater and allowing it to rise, he argued that if it was the shape that kept it afloat, surely this should not allow it to rise in this way. Cardinal Barberini eagerly took Galileo's side in this lively debate, and Galileo later put these thoughts into a book called *Discourse on Bodies that Stay Atop Water or Move Within It*. He wrote this while recovering from one of his recurring periods of illness at the villa of Filippo Salviati, who was a good friend. The book also contained his observations on sunspots and was written in Italian rather than the traditional Latin, so that it appealed to a wider audience.

Galileo then expanded his observations on sunspots in his *Letters on the Sunspots*, which was also published by the Lynceans. This is the only place where Galileo supports the Copernican system in writing when he states:

> With absolute necessity we shall conclude
> in agreement with the theories of the

Pythagoreans and of Copernicus, that Venus revolves about the Sun just as do all the other planets . . .

The book was published in March 1613, and it was not long before people began to criticize Galileo for the views he had voiced in this book.

GALILEO AND THE CATHOLIC CHURCH

1
2
3
4
5
7

CHAPTER 6

Matters began to become more difficult for Galileo in 1613. A former student of Galileo's, Benedetto Castelli, was invited to the Medici Palace in December for breakfast with Cosimo II and, among others, Cosimo's mother, Grand Duchess Christina of Lorraine. Christina asked Castelli whether the motion of Earth was contrary to the teaching of the Bible, in particular the book of Joshua where the Sun is ordered to stand still so Joshua has time to fight his battle. This, argued Christina, must surely mean that the Sun moved around Earth. Castelli argued this need not be the case and thought he had convinced her. However, Christina was a devout Catholic, and when Galileo heard about the event, he was not so sure of Castelli's victory. Galileo therefore sent

The spirit of the Counter-Reformation, the Catholic Church's response to Protestantism, was embodied in the Baroque period of art, which started in the seventeenth century. With its use of motion, color, and decoration, it symbolized a new expansive world view and was meant to evoke emotion for the church. Here, Saint Francis is baptizing new converts.

an immediate response, arguing that he believed Earth somehow drew its motion from the Sun, so if the Sun stopped rotating, Earth would also. Castelli copied Galileo's letter and shared it with many friends. It eventually found its way to a Catholic friar, Tommaso Caccini, who preached a sermon on December 21, 1614, condemning all mathematicians and, in particular, Galileo. This was the start of considerable trouble for Galileo.

Father Grienberger had succeeded Father Clavius at the Roman College and though he had initially accepted Galileo's arguments in December 1613, a letter was written by the general of the Jesuits, Claudio Aquaviva, insisting that Aristotelian natural philosophy be taught in the Jesuit schools. Father Grienberger had no choice but to follow this order and was unable to speak on Galileo's behalf. This was unfortunate as one friar, Niccolo Lorini, added to the growing problems of Galileo. Lorini had publicly attacked the Copernican theory in 1612, though, as he had wrongly given the name Ipernicus to Copernicus in his address, it was unlikely he had studied the work in depth. However, when Lorini got hold of a copy of Galileo's letter to Castelli in 1614, he found the contents so objectionable that he forwarded the letter to the Holy Office in Rome.

THE INQUISITION AND CONGREGATION OF INDEX

This was not an easy time to be questioning the church's reasoning. During the Middle Ages, knowledge had spread throughout the countries of western Europe under the control of the church. As people began to question the teachings during the Renaissance, the church was placed in a difficult position since it still wanted to hold on to this power of knowledge. When the Protestant Reformation occurred in Germany, the Catholic Church responded throughout the sixteenth and seventeenth centuries with the Counter-Reformation, hoping to bridge the gap between Catholicism and Protestantism, thus bringing religion back under the central control of Rome. A meeting of bishops, cardinals, and leaders of religious orders was called, which would become known as the Council of Trent. These men debated and voted on a draft of various decrees detailing how clergy members were to be educated, and insisted that no one should rely on their own judgment in interpreting the Bible. This process took about eighteen years, from 1545 to 1563. However, because the meetings took so long to arrange, the split between the Protestants and Catholics widened. The council also put in place an administrative system for

The Council of Trent was a major turning point in the Catholic Church's response to the Protestant Reformation. Reestablishing Catholic doctrine and directly opposing the growing Protestant movement, it sought to strengthen the church's traditions and sole right to interpret the Bible.

government called the Roman Curia and developed guidelines for discussions on science and religion.

Two congregations of the Roman Curia would be of great importance to Galileo. One of these was the

Holy Office, or Inquisition, whose role was to actively stop all opposition to the Catholic Church, by means of torture if necessary. It was hoped that all forms of Protestantism could be eliminated in Catholic areas. The second congregation that would affect Galileo was the Congregation of Index, which had the power to censor books. An index of forbidden books had existed for many years, but the Congregation of Index constantly checked and updated this list.

GALILEO INVESTIGATED

The Holy Office examined Galileo's letter to Castelli and Lorini's letter, which accompanied it on Wednesday, February 25, 1615. It was decided that the archbishop of Florence should obtain an original copy of Galileo's letter. At a further meeting on Thursday, March 19, 1615, Caccini, who had preached his sermon against Galileo, stirred up more trouble. He stated that not only had Galileo reported that the Sun stands still and Earth moves, but that he also had undesirable acquaintances, one of whom was Paolo Sarpi, Galileo's longtime friend from Venice. When the Holy Office met on Thursday, April 2, 1615, the pope decided to ask the Florentine inquisitor to interrogate two witnesses about

Caccini's claims. This evidence was heard on November 13 and 14, 1615, and concluded that Galileo was a good Catholic, but his *Letters on the Sunspots* should be considered in more detail. This was reported to a meeting of the Holy Office on Wednesday, November 25. Galileo was never charged with any offense and since these were regular meetings of the Holy Office, he was never even informed about the discussions. However, Galileo began to be increasingly concerned about what might have

The burning of books as a symbol of rejection of writers and their thoughts has existed since 213 BC. Here, Saint Dominic is depicted burning heretical works in 1501. The Congregation of Index lasted until 1948.

been passed as his letter to Castelli since so many copies were circulating. He decided to recast the letter into a more formal essay that became known as the "Letter to the Grand Duchess Christina of Lorraine." Though Galileo's letter to the Grand

Duchess Christina had accused his opponents of interpreting the Bible, something that the Council of Trent had said only the church could do, it could also be argued that Galileo was guilty of the same crime in this letter.

Galileo was a devout Catholic and was not trying to start a conflict between science and religion. He believed that the Bible was there to instruct people in how to get to heaven and was not meant to be a scientific book explaining how the universe worked. In his letter to Castelli, he states:

> I believe that the intention of Holy Writ was to persuade men of the truths necessary for salvation . . . Surely if the intention of the sacred scribes had been to teach the people astronomy, they would not have passed over the subject so completely.

He never saw a problem with various passages, which the church pointed out were contrary to the Copernican view of the universe. He was not alone in this view and in 1615, a priest named Paolo Antonio Foscarini published *A Letter on the Opinion of the Pythagorans and Copernicus Regarding the Motion of the Earth*. He argued that the Bible was compatible with the Copernican theory and even sent a copy of

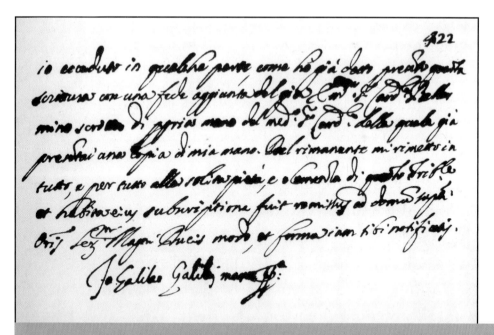

Above is the concluding section of Galileo's statement of his recantation, or confession, on June 22, 1633. The recantation did not include two points because Galileo was opposed to them: that he was not a good Catholic and that he had deceived others by publishing his book.

his book to Cardinal Bellarmine at the Holy Office. Bellarmine read the book and made it clear that he thought Copernicanism was fine in theory as long as it was used only as a hypothesis and not as an explanation for how the universe actually worked.

TREATISE ON TIDES

Galileo felt in danger of losing his good reputation and decided to visit Rome again. On December 11,

1615, he became the official guest of the Tuscan ambassador. He visited many cardinals and dignitaries, hoping to convince them of his claims. One particular convert was Alessandro Orsini, a cousin of Grand Duke Cosimo. Though Galileo's astronomical observations seemed to support a Copernican system, they did not provide proof that Earth moved. Galileo therefore looked elsewhere and came up with the theory that the tides must somehow be linked to the revolving Earth. He argued that the oceans could be thought of as a vessel of water on Earth, which rotates once a day (on its own axis) and travels around the Sun (revolves) once a year. Since these two motions are either in the same or opposite directions periodically, he believed this must make the waters flow in and out. If you fill a bucket with water and carry out these maneuvers, it does indeed make the water move in a tidelike way. Unfortunately, the tides have nothing to do with Earth's rotation. They are, in fact, caused by the Moon's gravity and could happen whether or not Earth is rotating. However, this was not known at the time. Orsini urged Galileo to put his theory in writing. Galileo did this in January in his *Treatise on Tides*, which was well thought out though unfortunately wrong.

Galileo entrusted his manuscript to Orsini to be passed on to Pope Paul V. The pope refused to read the document and instead asked Cardinal Bellarmine to set up a papal commission to decide once and for all whether or not Copernican ideas were heretical. The Holy Office asked a panel of eleven experts to consider firstly whether the Sun was the center of the universe and immovable, and secondly whether Earth moved. On February 24, 1616, when the cardinals met, not only did they decide that the ideas of the Sun being the center of the universe and Earth moving were heretical, but that they were also foolish and absurd.

GALILEO'S WARNING

The cardinals reported their finding back to the Holy Office and the pope promptly asked Bellarmine to tell Galileo that he could no longer hold or defend the Copernican views. If Galileo resisted this request of the Inquisition, then he would be told he could not hold, defend, or teach the system. The distinction between the two commands is of great importance for future events. If he could not teach the Copernican system, then he could not even discuss the system. If, however, Galileo did not object and the second command was not given, he would be able to discuss the system, providing it remained a hypothesis that he did not hold to be true.

Pope Paul V won the papacy over Galileo's good friend Bellarmine. Always defending the privileges of the church, Pope Paul V grew weary over the Galileo controversy. Eventually, he turned the matter over to the Holy Office.

On February 26, two officers of the Inquisition collected Galileo and escorted him to Cardinal Bellarmine. As was the custom, Bellarmine met Galileo at the door with his hat in his hand and had a quiet word with Galileo. It is believed that Bellarmine told Galileo not to object to anything that was said inside. The first order was given to Galileo when he entered the room, but before he had time to reply, the officers stepped in and issued the second warning also forbidding Galileo to teach the idea. Bellarmine was furious and escorted Galileo out telling him that he would be safe providing he obeyed the first order. The Inquisition, however, submitted an unsigned and unwitnessed record of the event stating that Galileo had agreed not to teach the Copernican system.

The following week, on March 1, five cardinals of the Congregation of Index met in Bellarmine's office, including Maffeo Barberini (who had taken Galileo's side in the staged debate over ice), to judge various works relating to the Copernican theory. On March 5, they published a proclamation stating that Copernican astronomy was false and contrary to Holy Scripture and suspended Copernicus's book until corrections to it were made. The only book banned outright was Foscarini's published *A Letter on the Opinion of the Pythagoreans and Copernicus Regarding the Motion of the Earth* as this had openly argued for the compatibility of the Bible and Copernicanism. Galileo's own book, *Letters on the Sunspots*, escaped any such dealings and since his *Letter to Grand Duchess Christina* and the *Treatise on the Tides* only existed in manuscript form, they also escaped.

Rumors now started to circulate around Italy that Galileo had been summoned to Rome and in some way charged with heresy. Galileo felt there was only one course of action to clear his name, and he appealed directly to Cardinal Bellarmine. Bellarmine explained to the pope the true nature of the February meeting and Pope Paul V granted Galileo a meeting on March 11, in which he told Galileo not to worry as long as he was pope. This did not stop rumors from spreading that the Inquisition had punished Galileo, so in May, Galileo asked Bellarmine for written evidence that he had simply been informed of the position the church took and had agreed to uphold this view. Bellarmine of course agreed, and Galileo returned to Florence in June, confident that he was safe.

THE TRIAL AND LATER YEARS

For the next couple of years, Galileo worked quietly, but he could not avoid controversy for long. In 1618, when three comets were sighted, he was urged by friends to give an opinion. Today we know that comets come from an icy cloud beyond the farthest planet, Pluto. Sometimes they leave this cloud and are attracted by the gravitational pull of the Sun. As they get closer to the Sun, heat causes the ice to evaporate and long tails are formed from the jets of dust and gas that are visible from Earth. Unfortunately, Galileo was bedridden with rheumatic pains when the comets were visible from November until January and was unable to observe the phenomena. He did, however, manage to reply to a published article written by a Jesuit mathematics professor at the Roman College, Father

According to Aristotelian cosmology, no change could occur among the heavens, only in the area between Earth and the Moon. Therefore, comets were wrongfully assumed to be located in that area for many centuries.

Orazio Grassi, who concluded that the comets were located between the Sun and the Moon. Galileo accused the Jesuits of spreading false information.

POPE URBAN VIII

On February 28, 1621, Cosimo died, leaving ten-year-old Ferdinando II as the new duke. Having someone so young in charge of the region seriously weakened any influence Tuscany had in Rome. Bellarmine's death in the same year left Galileo without a witness to the events of 1616. However, when Pope Paul V also died in 1621, a longtime friend of Galileo's, Cardinal Maffeo Barberini, became Pope Urban VIII. Galileo lost no time in dedicating his new book, *Il Saggiatore* (The Assayer), to the new pope. The book, which had grown out of his work on comets, was published in October 1623. Galileo wrote this book in a witty style and attacked the philosophers' methods of conducting science. One passage states:

Maffeo Barberini, Pope Urban VIII, enjoyed a long papacy that included such accomplishments as promoting missionary work; prohibiting slavery of the natives in Brazil, Paraguay, and the West Indies; and publishing several volumes of verse.

Philosophy is a book of fiction created by one man, like *The Iliad* . . . Philosophy is written in that great book which ever lies before our eyes—I mean the universe—but we cannot understand it if we do not first learn the language and grasp the symbols in which it is written. This book is written in mathematical language, and the symbols are triangles, circles, and other geometrical figures, without whose help it is humanly impossible to comprehend a single word of it, and without which one wanders in vain through a dark labyrinth.

Urban had the book read to him at mealtimes and is said to have roared with laughter over the attacks made on the philosophers.

After a long period of illness, Galileo eventually set out in April 1624 to pay his respects to Urban. The pope had six private meetings with him and by the time Galileo left in June, he had obtained permission to write a book about the two systems (Ptolemaic and Copernican) of the universe, providing he treated each system as a hypothesis. In other words, he was allowed to teach the Copernican system, but not defend it.

DIALOGUE CONCERNING THE TWO CHIEF WORLD SYSTEMS

Dialogue Concerning the Two Chief World Systems was finished in November 1629 and took the form of a four-day-long imaginary dialogue between two people with a third impartial observer. This provided a useful way to teach the Copernican idea without endorsing it. Galileo used two of his old friends, Filippo Salviati (who had died in 1614) to argue the Copernican system, and Giovanfrancesco Sagredo (an old Venetian friend who had helped Galileo with the dowry problems and had died in 1620) as the observer. A sixth-century Greek philosopher named Simplico had written a commentary on Aristotle, and Galileo used Simplico to argue the Ptolemaic system. The similarity of the name to "simpleton" could hardly go unnoticed.

The book had to be passed by a censor in Rome before publication. Niccolo Riccardi, a theologian from the Dominican order of the church, was assigned to this task, and Galileo delivered the book in May 1630. Although Riccardi wanted a new preface and conclusion added, he was happy with the work. The book was due to be published in Rome by the Lynceans, but Federico Cesi, the founder of the society, died in August 1630.

Galileo now decided to have the book printed in Florence. A Florentine reviewer was needed. Out of courtesy, Galileo contacted Riccardi to explain his position. Riccardi stated that he wanted to read the book again, but Galileo managed to reach a

DIALOGO

DI
GALILEO GALILEI LINCEO

MATEMATICO SOPRAORDINARIO

DELLO STVDIO DI PISA.

E Filoſofo, e Matematico primario del

SERENISSIMO

GR. DVCA DI TOSCANA.

Doue ne i congreſſi di quattro giornate ſi diſcorre
ſopra i due

MASSIMI SISTEMI DEL MONDO
TOLEMAICO, E COPERNICANO;

*Proponendo indeterminatamente le ragioni Filoſofiche, e Naturali
tanto per l'vna, quanto per l'altra parte.*

CON PRI VILEGI.

IN FIORENZA, Per Gio: Batiſta Landini MDCXXXII.

CON LICENZA DE' SVPERIORI.

This is the title page from Galileo's *Dialogue Concerning the Two Chief World Systems,* which was published in Florence in February 1632. Considered to be Galileo's masterpiece, it was placed on the Index of Prohibited Books following his 1633 trial. It remained there until 1835.

compromise by sending him only the changed preface and conclusion, which were then forwarded to Father Iacinto Stefani, the Florentine reviewer, in May 1631. The conclusion contained the views of the pope, stating science has limitations and God could have produced tides without setting Earth in motion in ways that men cannot imagine. These views were very close to the pope's heart, but unfortunately Galileo put them into the mouth of Simplico.

THE SUMMON TO ROME

The printing was completed in February 1632, and the first person in Rome to receive a copy of the dialogue was Cardinal Francesco Barberini, the pope's nephew, who wrote telling Galileo how much he enjoyed the book. Other people were less pleased with the book including Galileo's old enemy, Scheiner, and more important, Pope Urban.

There were two points that upset the pope: first, the altered preface had been put in a different typeface, suggesting that Galileo did not agree with the idea. Second, the conclusion that the Copernican system was a hypothesis as stated by Simplico suggested a simpleton had uttered the pope's words. A Commission of Enquiry was established to look at the book, and in September, an order reached

Florence forbidding any more sales. Unfortunately for the pope, it had already sold out! The commission recommended that the book be referred to the Holy Office and a meeting took place on September 23, where the report was discussed. A Florentine inquisitor was then instructed to summon Galileo to Rome.

Another bout of illness struck Galileo, who was now sixty-eight years old. His departure was delayed until January 20, 1633. Galileo eventually arrived in Rome on February 13 and was initially allowed to stay at the Tuscan Embassy. Here, the Tuscan ambassador explained that the pope had been given the unsigned record of the 1616 meeting stating Galileo could not teach the Copernican system.

GALILEO'S TRIAL

After two months of waiting, two officials, Commissioner Maculano and his assistant prosecutor, Carlo Sinceri, carried out the questioning on April 12. After questions concerning the writing, licensing, and printing of dialogue, attention turned to the 1616 meeting. Galileo was able to produce the letter from Bellarmine, but this was not enough. The commissioner had in his possession the unsigned minutes and asked whether Galileo had asked for

Above is an artist's depiction of Galileo's interrogation by the Inquisition. Galileo had been held in the building of the Inquisition for several weeks before the trial, at which time he promised to change his opinions about the Copernican system in his next work.

permission to write the book knowing he had been forbidden to teach the Copernican system. Galileo replied that he did not believe this was necessary since he had not intended to defend Copernicanism in his book. This was clearly not the case to anyone who had read the book, and Galileo now laid himself wide open to criticism.

The trial lasted for a considerable length of time, and at a meeting of the Holy Office on April 28,

Maculano suggested he should have a private meeting with Galileo to deal with the problem. Maculano persuaded Galileo to see that he had gone too far. When Galileo entered the commissioner's office on April 30 for a second formal hearing, he stated that he had re-read his manuscript and indeed thought certain parts of the book argued too forcefully for Copernicanism.

On May 10, Galileo handed over a written statement, which stated he had not knowingly disobeyed orders but was guilty only of vanity in wanting to appear clever. At Galileo's last summons on June 21, he stated that he had not held the Copernican theory since 1616 and he had merely written his dialogue to state the arguments for and against the system. The sentence was pronounced on June 22 that Galileo was suspected of heresy. Galileo was dressed in the white robe of penitent and knelt to read the statement written for him, claiming he did not believe in the Copernican system and his book had gone too far in presenting the Copernican case. Given the circumstance, it is unlikely that he uttered the words sometimes attributed to him, *eppu, si muove* (but it still moves). If this had been the case, his sentence would have probably been much harsher than the life imprisonment to which he was condemned along with the banning of his book.

Pictured above is Galileo's villa in Arcetri, near Florence. He came here to spend his time under house arrest, which lasted the remainder of his life. The home is near the convent of San Matteo, where Galileo's daughter Sister Maria Celeste lived.

Cardinal Barberini managed to get the sentence lightened so that the imprisonment was changed from the dungeons of the Holy Office to the Villa Medici and then to the arch-bishop of Siena's house. Finally at the beginning of 1634, Galileo was allowed to return home, though he remained under house arrest for the rest of his life.

This is an artist's depiction of Galileo under house arrest. The Inquisition allowed Galileo to attend religious services only on holidays.

GALILEO'S LATER LIFE

It was the archbishop of Siena who finally brought Galileo's mind back to science and persuaded him to complete his life's work on mechanics. This was again in the form of a dialogue between the same three friends over four days and entitled *Discourses and Mathematical Demonstrations Concerning Two New Sciences*. It took Galileo from 1634 to 1637 to complete the book. Rome had

Galileo petitioned the Inquisition various times to be released from house arrest for medical reasons. He was finally allowed to move to his home near Florence to be close to his doctors, by which time he was completely blind.

ruled that no book could be written or edited by Galileo, so his manuscript was smuggled to Holland and published in 1638. The book was enormously popular everywhere, except in Italy, and had a huge influence on modern science. It is no coincidence that from 1630, Italy lagged far behind the rest of the world in scientific discoveries. What had started with the Renaissance died due to the influence of the Catholic Church.

In October 1638, a sixteen-year-old scholar, Vincenzio Viviani, became Galileo's live-in companion. By this time, Galileo suffered from blindness. Viviani wrote and read Galileo's correspondences, helped him construct various scientific investigations, and became Galileo's first biographer.

Galileo died on the evening of January 8, 1642, just a few weeks short of his seventy-eighth birthday. At the time, he was beginning to dictate the start of a new dialogue between the three friends. He was buried in the Novices Chapel in Santa Croce, Florence, because Pope Urban had stopped Duke Ferdinando's plans to bury Galileo in the main church. Viviani tried all his life to move Galileo's tomb, but it was left to a distant relative of Viviani's to complete a tomb for Galileo in 1737. When the body was moved on March 12, 1737, a vertebra, three fingers of his right hand, and a tooth were removed as a symbol of his martyrdom. One of these fingers can still be seen in a crystal urn in the Institute and Museum of the History of Science in Florence.

CONCLUSION

The importance of Galileo to the scientific world cannot be overstated. His own accomplishments were

GALILAEVS GALILEIVS PATRIC. FLOR.
GEOMETRIAE ASTRONOMIAE PHILOSOPHIAE MAXIMVS RESTITVTOR
NVLLI AETATIS SVAE COMPARANDVS
HIC BENE QVIESCAT
VIX. A. LXXVIII. OBIIT. A. CIƆ. IƆ. C. XXXXI.
CVRANTIBVS AETERNVM PATRIAE DECVS
X. VIRIS PATRICIIS SACRAE HVIVS AEDIS PRAEFECTIS
MONIMENTVM A VINCENTIO VIVIANIO MAGISTRI CINERI SVIQVE SIMVL
TESTAMENTO F. I.
HERES IO. BAPT. CLEMENS NELLIVS IO. BAPT. SENATORIS F.
LVBENTI ANIMO ABSOLVIT.
AN. CIƆ. IƆ. CC XXXVII.

The tomb of Galileo Galilei is located in the Basilica of Santa Croce in Florence. The Catholic Church opposed the building of a monument to a man condemned of "vehement heresy." The removal of three fingers and a vertebra, which took place when he was moved to the tomb, was a gesture meant to emphasize his role as a hero and martyr of science.

enough to place him among the greatest scientists of history, but he also laid the foundation for later work. Isaac Newton continued Galileo's work, establishing his own laws of motion. When he combined these laws with his theory of gravitation, he was able to predict exactly how the planets moved around the Sun. Albert Einstein developed a complete theory of relativity over 200 years after Galileo first stated the idea in his *Dialogue Concerning the Two Chief World Systems.*

Most important, during the Renaissance, Galileo changed the way science was carried out. Never again would philosophy be the key to understanding. After Galileo's life, his scientific method of making observations and recording calculations would be the way forward for science. Though science progressed quickly, the Catholic Church was slower to change its attitudes. It was not until 1992 that Pope John Paul II made a public statement accepting Galileo's theories.

TIMELINE

1564   Galileo is born in Pisa on February 15.

1574   Galileo's family moves to Florence.

1579   Galileo is at the monastery of Santa Maria di Vallombrosa.

1581–1585   Galileo studies medicine at the University of Pisa.

1583   Galileo first formulates the pendulum law after watching the oscillations of a lamp in a Pisa cathedral.

1585   Galileo returns to Florence without a degree.

1585–1589   Galileo gives private lessons in Florence and Siena.

1586   Galileo constructs the hydrostatic balance.

1587   Galileo travels to Rome and meets Christoph Clavius.

1588   Galileo gives public lectures on Dante's *Inferno*.

1589   Galileo becomes professor of mathematics at the University of Pisa.

1591   Galileo drops weights from the Leaning Tower of Pisa to demonstrate the law of falling objects.

1597   Galileo invents the military compass.

1599   Galileo meets Marina Gamba.

1600   Galileo's daughter Virginia is born.

1601   Galileo's daughter Livia is born.

1604   Galileo experiments for the first time with rolling balls down an inclined plane.

1606   Galileo's son, Vincenzio, is born.

1608   Hans Lippershey invents the telescope.

1609   Galileo makes a telescope and uses it for a series of observations of the Moon.

TIMELINE [continued]

1610 Galileo is appointed chief mathematician of the University of Pisa and philosopher and mathematician to the grand duke of Tuscany. He observes the satellites of Jupiter and publishes *The Starry Messenger*.

1611 Galileo visits Rome to demonstrate the power of the telescope.

1613 Galileo publishes his *Letters on the Sunspots*.

1614 Thomas Caccini preaches his sermon against Galileo.

1615 Galileo meets Pope Paul V to discuss his theories of the universe.

1616 On February 24, the Holy Office decides that the idea of the Sun being the center of the universe and Earth rotating around it is heretical. On February 26, Ballarmine warns Galileo not to hold or defend the Copernican theory.

1618 Three comets appear.

1619 Galileo writes his *Discourse on the Comets*.

1620 The Congregation of Index issues corrections that must be made to Copernicus's *On the Revolutions*.

1621 Pope Paul V dies.

1623 *The Assayer* is published.

1624 Galileo has six audiences with Pope Urban VIII.

1632 *Dialogue Concerning the Two Chief World Systems* is published.

1633 Inquisition sentences Galileo to life imprisonment.

1634 Galileo returns home and remains under house arrest.

1638 *Two New Sciences* is published in Holland.

1642 Galileo dies on January 8.

GLOSSARY

apothecary One who prepares medicines.

cardinal The highest rank after pope in the Roman Catholic Church.

comet Lumps of ice, grit, and dust that move through the solar system. They form tails of gas as they approach the Sun.

concave Curved inward.

convex Curved outward.

density The amount of substance in a particular volume.

doge Chief magistrate of Venice.

dowry The money given by a bride's family to her husband when they marry.

excommunicate To ban someone from church or from taking Holy Communion (bread and wine).

fortification Defensive structures.

geometry The mathematical study of lines and surfaces.

heretical Holding views that are contrary to the teachings of the church.

lute A stringed instrument played with the fingers.

magnetism Ability of some materials to attract iron.

novice A candidate for admission to a monastery or the priesthood.

octave The eight notes above or below a given note.

patronage Financial support given to someone in order to encourage his or her artistic or scientific work.

philosopher Someone who studies or teaches theories on the nature and conduct of the world and universe.

plumb line A string weighted at one end, used to determine the vertical from a given point.

pope Bishop of Rome and head of the Roman Catholic Church.

supernova An explosion that increases the brightness of a star.

theologian Someone who studies religious beliefs.

triangulation A method of using a compass and map to fix a position.

universe The entire cosmos.

vacuum A place containing no matter and from which all air has been removed.

FOR MORE INFORMATION

Institute and Museum of the
  History of Science
Piazza de Giudici, 1
50122 Florence, Italy

Marshall Space Flight Center
One Tranquility Base
Huntsville, AL 35805
(256) 837-3400

WEB SITES

Due to the changing nature of Internet
links, the Rosen Publishing Group, Inc.,
has developed an online list of Web
sites related to the subject of this book.
This site is updated regularly. Please
use the link below to access this list:

http://www.rosenlinks.com/rsar/gaga

For Further Reading

Drake, Stillman. *Galileo: A Very Short Introduction.* Oxford, England: Oxford University Press, 2001.

Goldsmith, Mike. *Galileo Galilei* (Scientists Who Made History). London: Hodder Children's Books, 2001.

Gribbin, John, and Mary Gribbin. *Galileo in 90 Minutes.* London: Constable, 1997.

Gribbin, John. *Science: A History.* London: Penguin, 2002.

Sobel, Dava. *Galileo's Daughter. A Historical Memoir of Science, Faith and Love.* New York: Walker, 1999.

BIBLIOGRAPHY

Drake, Stillman. *Galileo at Work: His Scientific Biography*. Chicago: University of Chicago Press, 1978.

Galilei, Galileo. *Dialogue Concerning the Two Chief World Systems*. Translated by Stillman Drake. Berkeley, CA: University of California Press, 1967.

Galilei, Galileo. *Dialogue Concerning Two New Sciences*. Translated by Henry Crew and Alfonso de Salvio. New York: Dover, 1954.

Galilei, Galileo. *Letters on the Sunspots, Discoveries and Opinions of Galileo*. Translated by Stillman Drake. New York: Anchor, 1957.

Galilei, Galileo. *Letter to Grand Duchess Christina, Discoveries and Opinions of Galileo*. Translated by Stillman Drake. New York: Anchor, 1957.

Shea, William, and Mariano Artigas. *Galileo in Rome: The Rise and Fall of a Troublesome Genius*. Oxford, England: Oxford University Press, 2003.

Strathern, Paul. *The Medici: Godfathers of the Renaissance*. London: Jonathan Cape, 2003.

INDEX

About the Author

Having gained a Ph.D. in mathematics, Rachel Hilliam works both as an academic and statistical consultant. She has published several research papers and has given talks throughout the world.

Credits